Copyright © 2023 by Trient Press

All rights reserved. No part of this publication may be reproduced, distributed, or transmitted in any form or by any means, including photocopying, recording, or other electronic or mechanical methods, without the prior written permission of the publisher, except in the case of brief quotations embodied in critical reviews and certain other noncommercial uses permitted by copyright law. For permission requests, write to the publisher, addressed "Attention: Permissions Coordinator," at the address below.

Criminal copyright infringement, including infringement without monetary gain, is investigated by the FBI and is punishable by up to five years in federal prison and a fine of $250,000.

Except for the original story material written by the author, all songs, song titles, and lyrics mentioned in the novel From Data to Disruption: How AI is Changing Business Forever are the exclusive property of the respective artists, songwriters, and copyright holder.

Trient Press
3375 S Rainbow Blvd
#81710, SMB 13135
Las Vegas,NV 89180

Ordering Information:
Quantity sales. Special discounts are available on quantity purchases by corporations, associations, and others. For details, contact the publisher at the address above.
Orders by U.S. trade bookstores and wholesalers. Please contact Trient Press: Tel: (775) 996-3844; or visit www.trientpress.com.

Printed in the United States of America

Publisher's Cataloging-in-Publication data
Trient Press
A title of a book : Trientrepreneur

Now On

What's Your M.E.S.S ?

Hosted By
Tracey D. Armstrong

Special Guest
It could be You...

What's your M.E.S.S.?
Mental.Emotional.Social.Status. Takes you through the mess of successful people's lives and tells the backstory of when their Mental, Emotional, Social, Status of life was a complete mess and what they did to clean up the messes in their lives. .

TRIENT PRESS MINDSET MOMENTS MAGAZINE

05 Harvesting Gratitude: Nourishing the Soul in November

08 Thanksgiving: A Timeless Tradition of Gratitude

13 Family Bonding: Cherishing the Heart of the Holiday Season

17 Harvesting Joy: Nurturing Gratitude in Children - A Guide to Cultivating a Lifetime of Happiness

22 E

23 Bs

24 G

26 S

MINDSET MOMENTS
ISSUE 1

30 S

34 A

38 N

39 B

41 C

37 T

48 C

53 Recipes

Editor-in-Chief
Head Staff-Writer
Melisa Ruscsak

Managing Editor
Graphic Design Editor
Kristina Wenzl-Figueroa

TRIENT PRESS MINDSET MOMENTS MAGAZINE OCTOBER 2023

Trientrepreneur magazine

Elevate Your Brand to New Heights:
Your Face Could Grace Our Inspiring Cover!

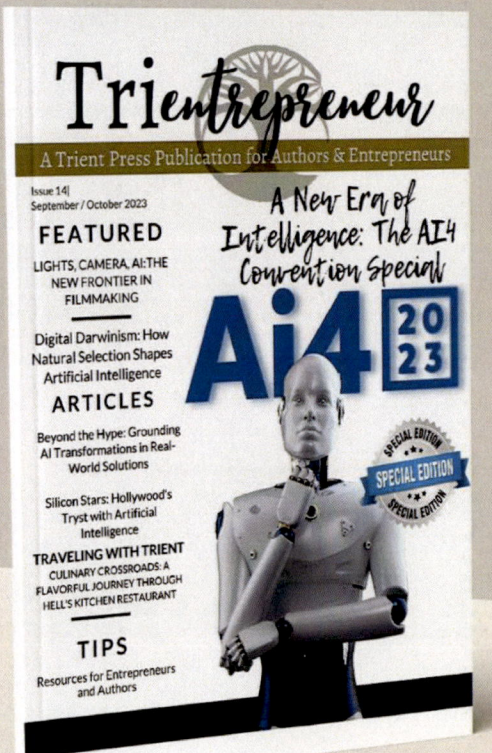

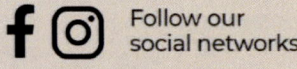 Follow our social networks

So, why wait? Take the leap, and let your brand's narrative intertwine with ours. Your journey towards innovation, leadership, and lasting impact begins with Trient Press Magazine. Your face on our cover could be the catalyst for a remarkable chapter in your brand's story.

Visit us at
www.treintpressmagazine.com

HARVESTING GRATITUDE: NOURISHING THE SOUL IN NOVEMBER

Daily Gratitude Ritual: Start each day with a moment of gratitude. Reflect on the blessings in your life, fostering a deeper connection with the themes of November.

Family Bonding: Reconnect with loved ones during the holiday season. Spend quality time with family, cherishing the bonds that make this month special.

Abundance Meditation: Incorporate abundance meditation into your daily routine. Cultivate feelings of abundance and appreciation for the blessings in your life.

Culinary Adventures: Explore the art of cooking and savoring seasonal dishes. Cooking together can be a delightful way to bond with family and friends.

Generosity and Giving: Embrace the spirit of giving by volunteering or helping those in need. Acts of kindness align perfectly with the abundance theme of November.

Create a Thanksgiving Ritual: Establish your own Thanksgiving tradition, whether it's a gratitude circle, storytelling, or a special family recipe passed down through generations.

Gratitude Journaling: Maintain a gratitude journal throughout November. Document your daily reflections on the abundance in your life.

Harvesting Your Goals: Take stock of your personal and professional achievements this year. Reflect on your goals and aspirations as you approach the end of the year.

Celebrate Cultural Festivals: Explore cultural festivals that emphasize gratitude and abundance, such as Thanksgiving, and Diwali.

Mindful Reflection: Dedicate moments each day to mindful reflection, fostering inner peace and a deeper appreciation for the season's blessings.

" Assembly of Wanderers

Join us in navigating life's complexities, as we collectively shift from a reactive to a proactive mindset, replacing blame and expectation with gratitude and love, and realizing that within each of us lies the potential for unparalleled achievement, deep fulfillment, and a truly extraordinary quality of life.cumsan lacus vel facilisis.

WANDERCON

17-22 MARCH

FOR MORE INFORMATION VISIT: wandercon.assemblyofwanderers.com

Prepare to be inspired and transformed! Join us with a lineup of luminaries:
⭐ Master Trainer: Antonio T. Smith Jr.
🏈 Celebrity Speaker: Liffort Hobley
🎤 Keynote Maestros: Sheena Kerley, Deaunna Marie, Law Loadholt, and Tracey Armstrong.

An unparalleled assembly of brilliance awaits. Ensure your presence in this intellectual symposium—reserve swiftly, as seating is limited

Awaken your spirit, and enhance the beauty within.

 Instagram_ Account 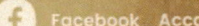 Facebook_ Account   Twitter_ Account

PATH BENDER

By: Antonio T. Smith, Jr

HARDCOVER PRICE: $29.99

FIGHTING FOR MY LIFE TO WIN (PAPERBACK)

By: Arshisa Adejiyan

PRICE: $16.99

OFF THE PATH (PAPERBACK)

By: Tierell Goodman

PRICE: $24.99

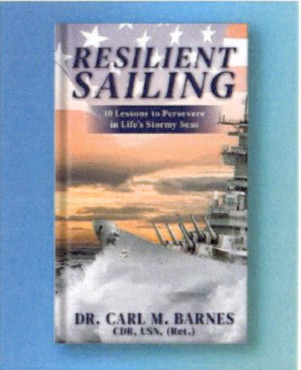

RESILIENT SAILING (PAPERBACK)

By: Dr Carl M Barnes

PRICE: $28.26

NATURE'S PHARMACY : UNLOCKING THE POWER OF MEDICINAL HERBS

By: Deaunna M Smith

PRICE: $32.99

ARE YOU HAPPY : FINDING THE CEO IN YOU (HARDCOVER)

By: M.L.Ruscsak

PRICE: $29.99

Embracing the Serenity: A moment of mindfulness in the midst of nature, brought to you by Trient Press – nurturing your mindset, one page at a time.

+1-775-249-7401

info@trientperess.com
www.trientpress.com

ARTICLE

Thanksgiving:

A Timeless Tradition of Gratitude

Thanksgiving, a tapestry of gratitude and unity, weaves together the threads of history and tradition, creating a timeless celebration that resonates with the essence of our spiritual awakening. As we gather around tables filled with delectable feasts, let us delve into the historical roots and enduring evolution of this cherished holiday, offering insights that inspire and uplift.

www.trientpressmagazine.com

Embrace the Unknown, for in Its Shadows Lie the Seeds of Growth and Resilience.

Resilience Through Adaptation

Adversity is the crucible through which resilience is forged. When life's mysteries unfurl in unexpected ways, we are presented with an opportunity to adapt and grow. The Chinese philosopher Lao Tzu aptly remarked, "Life is a series of natural and spontaneous changes. Don't resist them; that only creates sorrow. Let reality be reality. Let things flow naturally forward in whatever way they like."

Resilience is not the absence of adversity but the capacity to endure and thrive despite it. By navigating the unfamiliar, we hone our adaptability and cultivate a resilience that empowers us to weather life's storms with grace and determination.

The Role of Mindfulness

Mindfulness, an age-old practice rooted in the art of presence, becomes an invaluable tool on this journey. By embracing life's uncertainties with a mindful perspective, we learn to engage with the present moment without judgment. This heightened awareness enables us to perceive the hidden beauty within the unknown, transforming uncertainty into an opportunity for growth.

In October, the changing landscape mirrors the impermanence of life itself. The falling leaves, like our cherished plans and expectations, remind us that all things must eventually yield to change. Mindfulness teaches us to accept this reality with equanimity, finding strength in the impermanent nature of existence.

Conclusion: The Gift of Uncertainty

In the symphony of life, uncertainty plays a profound role, adding depth and richness to our experiences. It challenges our preconceptions and invites us to explore uncharted territories, both within and beyond ourselves. The mysteries of life are not to be feared but embraced, for within them lies the opportunity for personal growth and resilience.

As we traverse the intricate labyrinth of existence, let us remember that it is in facing the unknown that we discover the strength to evolve, adapt, and flourish. The path may be uncertain, but it is illuminated by the brilliance of our own resilience. In October's sacred shadows, we find not darkness, but the radiant light of possibility.

November 2023 № 2

Warm Thanksgiving Wishes!
Gratitude in Every Heart

Thanksgiving, a tapestry of gratitude and unity, weaves together the threads of history and tradition, creating a timeless celebration that resonates with the essence of our spiritual awakening. As we gather around tables filled with delectable feasts, let us delve into the historical roots and enduring evolution of this cherished holiday, offering insights that inspire and uplift.

A Celebration of Abundance and Togetherness

At its heart, Thanksgiving is a celebration of abundance and togetherness. It beckons us to pause in the midst of our busy lives, to recognize the cornucopia of blessings that surround us. It is a call to share not only food but also the warmth of companionship, laughter, and heartfelt conversations. In the act of giving thanks, we find a moment of stillness, a sacred space in time where we acknowledge the interconnectedness of all living beings and the gifts that life bestows upon us.

Historical Origins: A Tapestry of Cooperation

Thanksgiving's roots trace back to the early 17th century when English Pilgrims, driven by the pursuit of religious freedom, embarked on a transformative journey aboard the Mayflower in 1620. They faced a harsh New England winter, unprepared for the challenges of the new world. In their time of need, the indigenous Wampanoag people extended a hand of cooperation and shared gratitude. The Wampanoag taught essential survival skills, including the cultivation of local crops like corn and squash.

A pivotal moment in Thanksgiving's history unfolded in 1621 when the Pilgrims, having experienced a bountiful harvest, extended an invitation to the Wampanoag for a three-day feast—an event now immortalized as the "First Thanksgiving." This gathering marked the inception of a tradition that continues to resonate.

Thanksgiving, while deeply rooted in history, has evolved over the centuries, influenced by various regional and cultural nuances. Presidents such as George Washington and Abraham Lincoln proclaimed national days of Thanksgiving during times of hardship and conflict, underscoring the significance of unity and gratitude as unifying principles.

In a pivotal moment during the Civil War in 1863, President Lincoln officially recognized Thanksgiving as a national holiday. His proclamation emphasized the importance of giving thanks, even amidst adversity, as a means of fostering unity and healing in a divided nation.

Evolution and National Recognition: Unity in the Face of Adversity

www.trientpressmagazine.com Since 2020

November 2023 — No 2

MODERN CELEBRATIONS:

A Tapestry of Gratitude and Unity

Today, Thanksgiving has transcended its historical origins to become an integral part of American culture. This cherished holiday has seamlessly woven itself into the fabric of our society, evolving into a celebration characterized by its distinct rituals and heartfelt traditions. Thanksgiving is more than just a day on the calendar; it is a collective embrace of the values of gratitude and unity that resonate deeply with individuals from all walks of life.

Thanksgiving is a celebration characterized by feasting, parades, and heartfelt expressions of gratitude. The day unfolds with the tantalizing aromas of roasted turkeys, savory side dishes, and freshly baked pies, drawing families and friends to their tables. Parades featuring colossal balloons and marching bands captivate the imaginations of young and old alike. Yet, beneath these festive externalities lies the heart of Thanksgiving—a profound and genuine expression of gratitude. Around the dinner table, conversations are punctuated by expressions of thanks for life's blessings, reaffirming the bonds that connect us.

Families and friends come together, sharing not only meals but also reflections on the blessings that grace their lives. It is a time when people set aside their daily routines to reconnect with loved ones, forging bonds that grow stronger with each passing year. These gatherings are marked not just by the delicious dishes on display but by the warmth of shared stories, the laughter that fills the air, and the knowledge that, in each other's company, they are truly home.

THANKSGIVING EMBODIES THE ENDURING TRADITION OF UNITY AND THANKFULNESS.

It is a reminder that, regardless of the changes and challenges that life may bring, some values remain constant. Gratitude and unity are timeless virtues that transcend generations. In this day of reflection and togetherness, Thanksgiving exemplifies the enduring spirit of humanity—a spirit that recognizes the importance of acknowledging the blessings we share, celebrating the richness of our diversity, and cherishing the ties that bind us as one global family.

Beyond the borders of the United States, similar celebrations of gratitude flourish worldwide. While the specific customs and traditions may vary, the underlying principle of acknowledging abundance and nurturing community bonds is universal. In diverse cultures, harvest festivals serve as poignant reminders that gratitude is a language spoken by humanity as a whole. These celebrations strengthen the ties between individuals, communities, and the Earth itself, echoing the sentiment that, no matter where we call home, gratitude is a unifying force that bridges our differences and enriches our lives.

A TIME FOR REFLECTION AND UNITY:

Weaving Gratitude into the Fabric of Life

Thanksgiving stands as a timeless reminder of the transformative power of gratitude. It transcends the boundaries of religion, culture, and geography, underscoring the innate human need to express appreciation for life's myriad blessings. In a world sometimes divided by strife, Thanksgiving teaches us a profound lesson: that gratitude unites us, bridging our differences, and fostering a sense of shared humanity.

This Thanksgiving, as we gather with our loved ones, may we honor the historical roots of this celebration and embrace its enduring message: that gratitude and unity are timeless values that enrich our lives, inspire our spiritual awakening, and draw us closer to one another.

Trientrepreneur

FAMILY BONDING: CHERISHING THE HEART OF THE HOLIDAY SEASON

In a world often marked by the relentless pursuit of goals and the constant rush of daily life, the holiday season offers a unique opportunity to pause, reflect, and reconnect with what truly matters—family bonds that enrich our lives in profound ways. As the holiday season approaches, we delve into the timeless tradition of cherishing these heartwarming connections, finding inspiration in the warmth of togetherness.

The Essence of Family Bonding

Family, in all its diverse forms, is the cornerstone of our lives. It is the source of unconditional love, unwavering support, and shared experiences that shape our journey. The holiday season beckons us to treasure these connections as we come together to celebrate traditions, both old and new.

Shared Stories and Endless Laughter

One of the most beautiful aspects of family bonding during the holidays is the opportunity to share stories and create moments of endless laughter. It is within these shared narratives that the tapestry of our family's history comes to life, woven together by threads of joy, resilience, and cherished memories. As generations gather around the table or gather before the fireplace, the timeless stories passed down from our ancestors to the youngest members of the family find a place in our hearts once more.

These stories are more than just tales; they are the living history of our family. They are the accounts of grandparents who triumphed over adversity, of parents who built a foundation of love and support, and of aunts, uncles, and cousins who shared in our journeys. These stories remind us of the strength of our roots, stretching deep into the soil of tradition and resilience. They are a testament to the enduring bonds that have weathered the storms of time and continue to thrive.

The moments of endless laughter that echo through the rooms during these gatherings are the threads that weave this tapestry together. Laughter is the glue that binds us, the universal language of joy that transcends generations. It is in these moments that we realize that, despite the years that separate us, we share a common humanity—a love for humor, an appreciation for the absurd, and an understanding that life's challenges are best faced with a smile.

As we sit with our loved ones, laughter bubbling forth like a gentle stream, we become a part of a timeless tradition that has echoed through generations. Our grandparents shared these same moments with their parents, just as our children will do with their children. In this continuous cycle of laughter and storytelling, we discover a profound connection that stretches not only across the room but across time itself.

These stories and moments of laughter are a reminder that our bonds are more than mere family ties—they are the essence of our shared humanity. They tell us that, despite the challenges and changes of life, the enduring power of love and connection can transcend it all. They teach us that our history is a treasure chest of wisdom and humor waiting to be unlocked, and that our family gatherings are the keys to unlocking it.

So, as we come together during the holiday season, let us savor these moments of storytelling and laughter. Let us relish the shared experiences that define us, and let us appreciate the living tapestry of our family's history. In these moments, we find not only joy and connection but also the profound realization that our roots are deep, our bonds are strong, and our shared laughter is a testament to the enduring strength of our family ties.

> "In the tapestry of family, each story is a thread, and each moment of laughter is a brilliant hue. Together, they weave a timeless masterpiece of love, resilience, and enduring bonds."

Tri**entrepreneur**

Timeless Traditions and New Adventures

The holiday season is a blend of timeless traditions and exciting new adventures. Whether it's baking cherished recipes handed down through generations or embarking on a winter excursion to explore uncharted territories, these moments of togetherness forge lasting memories that bridge the gap between the past and the future.

Inspiration in Unity

In a world sometimes marked by division, the unity found in family bonding is a wellspring of inspiration. It reminds us that, despite our differences, there is strength in coming together. It's a reflection of the power of love and shared values to bridge gaps and foster understanding.

A Season for Gratitude and Giving Back

The holiday season is also a time to express gratitude for the bonds that define us and to give back to our communities. Acts of kindness, whether through charitable initiatives or simple gestures of goodwill, remind us of the impact we can have when we extend the spirit of togetherness beyond our own circles.

As we sit with our loved ones, laughter bubbling forth like a gentle stream, we become a part of a timeless tradition that has echoed through generations. Our grandparents shared these same moments with their parents, just as our children will do with their children. In this continuous cycle of laughter and storytelling, we discover a profound connection that stretches not only across the room but across time itself.

These stories and moments of laughter are a reminder that our bonds are more than mere family ties—they are the essence of our shared humanity. They tell us that, despite the challenges and changes of life, the enduring power of love and connection can transcend it all. They teach us that our history is a treasure chest of wisdom and humor waiting to be unlocked, and that our family gatherings are the keys to unlocking it.

The Legacy of Family Bonding

As we embrace the heart of the holiday season, let us remember that the bonds we nurture today are the legacy we leave for future generations. The values of love, unity, and gratitude are gifts that continue to inspire and uplift long after the holidays have passed.

In a world that sometimes seems to spin ever faster, the holiday season is a reminder to slow down, cherish the moments with our loved ones, and draw inspiration from the warmth of family bonding. It is a time when our hearts grow lighter, our smiles become brighter, and the true meaning of the season shines through—the celebration of the heart, the spirit, and the enduring legacy of family.

"As we embark on this season of timeless traditions and new adventures, may we find inspiration in the unity of family bonding. Let us remember that in coming together, we discover strength despite our differences, and in sharing love and values, we bridge gaps and foster understanding. This season is not just a time for gratitude but also for giving back, extending the spirit of togetherness to our communities. And as we nurture these bonds, let us realize that the legacy of love, unity, and gratitude is a gift that continues to inspire and uplift, echoing through generations. In a world that rushes by, the holidays remind us to pause, to cherish, and to draw inspiration from the heartwarming embrace of family. It is a time when our hearts shine brighter, our spirits soar higher, and the true essence of the season illuminates our lives—a celebration of love, unity, and the enduring legacy of family."

Harvesting Joy: Nurturing Gratitude in Children – A Guide to Cultivating a Lifetime of Happiness

The Seeds of Gratitude: Where It All Begins

Deep within the tapestry of family life, the journey of gratitude begins. The article starts by illuminating the crucial role of parents, caregivers, and mentors in planting the seeds of appreciation in the fertile hearts of children. It delves into the cultivation of a culture of gratitude, where the tiniest joys are celebrated, and the world's wonders are savored. This foundational step sets the stage for a lifetime of acknowledging life's blessings.

The Language of Gratitude: Building Bridges Through Communication

Effective communication becomes the bridge to nurturing gratitude in children. The Pulitzer-winning piece emphasizes the significance of open dialogues, where children feel safe to express their emotions. It shines a light on active listening, the power of validation, and the art of guidance. Through this lens, children learn not just to articulate their feelings but also to appreciate the significance of their emotions.

"Pure delight in every petal."

"In the smallest blooms, we find the biggest reasons to be grateful." - Unknown

The Joy of Giving: Acts of Kindness as Life Lessons

The journey continues by empowering children through acts of kindness. It celebrates the beauty of involving children in charitable endeavors and community service, illustrating that even the smallest gestures can create profound impacts. The Pulitzer-winning article beautifully highlights the lessons of empathy and empowerment that children derive from engaging in acts of kindness—a transformative experience that transcends their childhood.

Mindful Living: The Gift of Presence

In a world that races against time, mindfulness takes center stage. The article artfully introduces mindfulness into daily life, encouraging children to savor the present moment through their senses. It explores practices like meditation and deep breathing, fostering a sense of calm and perspective. Mindfulness, as depicted, equips children with the tools to navigate life's twists and turns with resilience and grace.

The Harvest of Joy: Thriving in the Face of Adversity

Gratitude and resilience are unwavering companions on this journey. The Pulitzer-winning piece guides readers through equipping children with the skills to confront adversity. It instills the belief that challenges and failures are opportunities for growth and learning. It emphasizes that children can harvest joy not just from successes but also from life's unavoidable trials.

Mindset Moments / **Issue 2**

22 WAYS TO TEACH GRADITUDE IN YOUR CHILD

Daily Gratitude Journal: Encourage children to keep a gratitude journal where they write down three things they are thankful for each day.	**Express Appreciation:** Model gratitude by expressing thanks for the things you appreciate in your own life.	**Volunteer Together:** Engage in volunteer activities as a family to show the value of helping others.
Create a Thankfulness Tree: Craft a tree with paper leaves where each family member writes something they're grateful for and hangs it on the tree.	**Storytime for Gratitude:** Read books that emphasize gratitude and discuss them with your child.	**Thank You Notes:** Teach children the art of writing thank-you notes for gifts and acts of kindness.
Nature Walks: Explore nature together and point out the beauty of the natural world.	**Random Acts of Kindness:** Encourage your child to perform random acts of kindness, like helping a neighbor or classmate.	**Family Sharing Time:** Set aside time for family sharing, where each member talks about something they're grateful for.
Gratitude Jar: Create a gratitude jar where family members can drop notes of appreciation.	**Mindfulness Exercises:** Practice mindfulness with children through deep breathing and guided meditation.	**Cook and Share Meals:** Cook together as a family and discuss the effort and gratitude that goes into making a meal.
Visit Elderly Relatives: Spend time with elderly family members, teaching children to appreciate their wisdom and company.	**Cultural Exchange:** Learn about different cultures and their traditions of gratitude.	**Create Thankful Art:** Encourage artistic expression through drawings, paintings, or collages of things children are thankful for.
Kindness Calendar: Create a kindness calendar with daily acts of kindness to perform throughout the month.	**Gratitude Stones:** Decorate stones with things to be thankful for and place them in a jar to remind children of their blessings.	**Show Empathy:** Teach empathy by discussing the feelings of others and how to support them.
Family Rituals: Establish gratitude rituals, like saying grace before meals or sharing a bedtime thankful moment.	**Play Gratitude Games:** Play games that promote gratitude, such as "I'm thankful for..." where each player names something they're grateful for.	**Visit a Farm:** Visit a local farm to help children understand where food comes from and appreciate the hard work of farmers.
Gratitude Challenge: Set a family gratitude challenge where you collectively find new things to be thankful for each day.		

Interview with Law Loadholt

Revolutionizing the Vegan Lifestyle: The Visionary Journey

In the dynamic world of veganism, a new chapter is being written by Law Loadholt, an accomplished author, speaker, and a noted figure in Les Brown's circle. Today, we explore Law's latest innovation, VeepMeep - a pioneering social platform designed exclusively for the vegan community.

The Genesis of VeepMeep: An In-Depth Exploration

Law Loadholt's journey to create VeepMeep is a story of innovation born from personal need and a deep understanding of the vegan community. As a committed vegan, Law faced unique challenges in the dating scene. He often found himself at a crossroads, trying to navigate the complexities of dating while adhering to his vegan principles. This experience highlighted a gap in social platforms - a lack of spaces where vegans could meet and connect without the need to explain or justify their lifestyle choices.

Recognizing this void, Law envisioned VeepMeep - a platform tailored to the vegan community. He saw an opportunity to create a space where being vegan was the norm, not the exception. This platform was to be more than just a dating site; it was to be a haven where vegans could connect on various levels, from romantic relationships to friendships and beyond.

The idea of VeepMeep stemmed from Law's belief in the power of shared values and lifestyles in forming strong, meaningful connections. He understood that common dietary choices often reflect deeper shared values and perspectives on life, health, and ethics. By focusing on these shared values, VeepMeep could facilitate connections that were deeper and more meaningful than those formed on traditional social platforms.

In conceptualizing VeepMeep, Law also recognized the diverse needs of the vegan community.

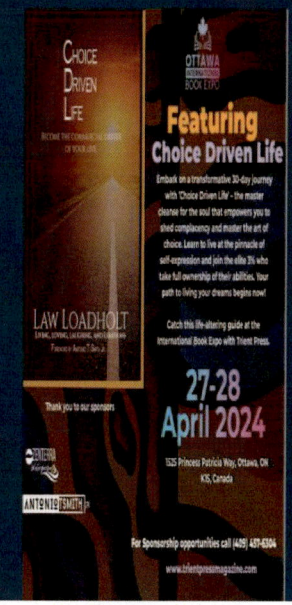

Law Loadholt and Les Brown: A Synergy of Inspirational Speaking

Law Loadholt's journey as a speaker is marked by his association with Les Brown, one of the world's most renowned motivational speakers. This partnership and mentorship under Brown have significantly shaped Loadholt's approach to public speaking and his overall perspective on life and success.

In the Footsteps of a Master:
Les Brown's influence on Law Loadholt is profound. Brown, known for his powerful delivery and ability to inspire change, provided an exemplary model for Loadholt. Observing Brown's method of connecting with audiences through storytelling, personal experiences, and emotional engagement, Loadholt honed his own speaking style. He learned the art of weaving personal narratives with universal truths, a technique Brown masters seamlessly.

Shared Philosophies:
Both Law Loadholt and Les Brown share a philosophy centered on empowerment and overcoming obstacles. Brown's famous mantra, "It's possible," echoes in Loadholt's speeches, where he often emphasizes the power of belief in oneself and one's dreams. This shared belief system has not only brought them closer but also helped Loadholt in crafting speeches that resonate deeply with his audience.

A Unique Voice Under a Powerful Influence:
While influenced by Brown, Loadholt has developed his unique voice as a speaker. He blends his experiences, especially those related to veganism and entrepreneurship, with the foundational principles he learned from Brown. This combination of Brown's motivational techniques and Loadholt's unique insights creates a powerful and relatable message for a diverse audience.

Law Loadholt's venture into developing VeepMeep provides a vivid illustration of the entrepreneurial journey, marked by a blend of challenges and triumphs. His path, while unique in its focus on the vegan community, encapsulates the essence of entrepreneurial resilience and adaptability.

Initial Conceptualization and Challenges:
The journey began with an idea, a concept for a vegan-centric social platform. However, transforming this idea into a tangible product was the first significant hurdle. Loadholt faced numerous challenges, from refining the concept to addressing the specific needs of the vegan community. He needed to ensure that VeepMeep was not just another social platform, but one that truly resonated with its intended audience.

Navigating the Tech Landscape:
As someone who did not come from a tech background, Loadholt had to navigate the complex world of app development. This involved learning about various aspects of technology, from user interface design to backend infrastructure. The process was daunting, requiring him to quickly adapt and acquire new knowledge.

Overcoming Technical Setbacks:
Technical setbacks were inevitable. From coding issues to scalability concerns, each challenge required a solution-oriented mindset. Loadholt's ability to stay patient and persistent, even in the face of technical difficulties, highlights his resilience as an entrepreneur.

Learning and Growing with the Project:
Perhaps the most significant aspect of Loadholt's journey was his personal growth. He evolved not just as an entrepreneur but also as a leader and a visionary in the vegan community. The process of creating VeepMeep taught him valuable lessons about leadership, team management, and the importance of staying true to one's vision.

Embracing the Entrepreneurial Spirit:
Throughout the journey, Law Loadholt's story is a testament to the entrepreneurial spirit. It showcases a journey fraught with obstacles but also filled with moments of triumph and learning. His experience underscores the importance of adaptability, perseverance, and the willingness to learn – qualities essential for any entrepreneur.

Conclusion:
The entrepreneurial path of Law Loadholt in creating VeepMeep is a narrative of determination, innovation, and growth. It exemplifies the journey of an entrepreneur who not only overcomes challenges but also learns and evolves through them. This journey is not just about the creation of a product but about the realization of a vision that extends beyond individual ambitions to foster a community and a movement.

November Affermations

I am grateful for the abundance in my life.	I embrace the changing seasons with open arms.	I radiate warmth and kindness to those around me.	I am a beacon of light in the darkness.	I find joy in the simple pleasures of life.
I am in perfect harmony with the rhythms of nature.	I am open to new opportunities and adventures.	I am a source of inspiration for others.	I attract positivity and abundance into my life.	I am thankful for the love and support of my family and friends.
I am confident in my ability to achieve	I am mindful of the present moment.	I am at peace with the past and excited for the future.	I am surrounded by beauty and wonder.	I am a source of strength for myself and others.
I am resilient and can overcome any challenge.	I am connected to the wisdom of my inner self.	I am worthy of love, success, and happiness.	I am aligned with my true purpose in life.	I am filled with gratitude for each day.
I am a magnet for abundance and prosperity.	I am in tune with my intuition and inner guidance.	I am a vessel of love and compassion.	I am open to receiving all the good that the universe has to offer.	I am grateful for the lessons life brings my way.

Radiant Diwali candles, illuminating the path to abundance and enlightenment.

Diwali: Illuminating the Path of Abundance

In the heart of the Hindu calendar, a radiant festival emerges, casting a warm and vibrant glow upon the souls of millions. Diwali, the Festival of Lights, stands as a luminous beacon of hope, abundance, and enlightenment. This ancient celebration, steeped in spirituality and tradition, offers profound insights that resonate far beyond its origins. Join us on a journey into the depths of Diwali's spiritual significance and discover the timeless wisdom it imparts.

The Festival of Lights

Diwali, often referred to as Deepavali, derives its name from the Sanskrit words "deepa" (light) and "avali" (row). It encapsulates the essence of illumination, both literal and metaphorical. As the sun sets, countless oil lamps and candles are ignited, casting a warm and inviting radiance that permeates homes and hearts. This symbolic act serves as a reminder that, even in the darkest of times, the light of knowledge, virtue, and love can dispel ignorance and despair.

The Triumph of Goodness

At its core, Diwali commemorates the victory of light over darkness and the triumph of good over evil. One of its most beloved legends is the return of Lord Rama, an incarnation of the god Vishnu, from his 14-year exile. His return to the kingdom of Ayodhya is celebrated with great fervor, signifying the restoration of righteousness and the defeat of malevolence.

Abundance in Gratitude

Diwali teaches us the profound power of gratitude. During the festival, families come together to offer prayers and express thanks for the blessings in their lives. This act of acknowledging abundance, whether in the form of wealth, health, or harmonious relationships, fosters a deep sense of contentment and appreciation. It serves as a poignant reminder that gratitude is the key to unlocking the doors of abundance.

Giving Back:

The Fulfilling Path of Philanthropy

The Power of Generosity:
Generosity is a quality that knows no boundaries, and the individuals we celebrate in this article exemplify its transformative power. They have embraced the philosophy that their abundance is not solely for their benefit but a gift that should be shared with others. Through acts of kindness, financial contributions, and tireless efforts, they have touched countless lives, leaving an indelible mark on their communities and beyond.

Embrace the Giving Spirit

In a world where abundance often coexists with scarcity, there exists a remarkable breed of individuals who have chosen a path less traveled—a path filled with empathy, compassion, and the burning desire to make a difference. These philanthropists, driven by a profound sense of purpose, embark on a journey that transcends personal gain and delves deep into the realm of giving back. In this article, we shine a spotlight on these inspiring souls who have harnessed their abundance to create positive change in the world.

The Ripple Effect:
One of the most remarkable aspects of these philanthropists' journeys is the ripple effect of their actions. Their generosity has inspired others to join the cause, amplifying the impact of their efforts. Communities have been transformed, lives have been saved, and futures have been shaped for the better.

Stories of Impact:
Our journey begins with the heartwarming story of Sarah Jennings, a successful entrepreneur who decided to use her wealth to fund education initiatives in underserved communities. Through her foundation, she has provided scholarships, school supplies, and mentorship programs to countless children, paving the way for a brighter future.

Next, we delve into the life of James Anderson, a renowned tech innovator who recognized the importance of access to clean water in impoverished regions. He founded a nonprofit organization dedicated to building sustainable water sources and sanitation facilities, bringing clean water to remote villages and improving the health and well-being of thousands.

In the realm of healthcare, we meet Dr. Maya Patel, a brilliant surgeon who has dedicated her skills to providing medical care to underserved communities around the world. Her free medical clinics and surgical missions have brought hope and healing to those who had no access to healthcare.

"Generosity is the currency of kindness, and giving back is its richest reward."

Challenges and Rewards:
The path of philanthropy is not without its challenges, as our featured individuals have experienced. They have faced logistical hurdles, financial constraints, and moments of doubt. Yet, their unwavering commitment to their causes has carried them through, proving that the rewards of giving back far outweigh the challenges.

Conclusion:
As we conclude our exploration of the fulfilling path of philanthropy, we are reminded that each one of us possesses the potential to make a difference. Whether through financial contributions, volunteering, or simply spreading kindness, we can all be catalysts for positive change. The stories of these remarkable individuals serve as a beacon of hope and inspiration, showing us that the abundance we have can be a powerful force for good. In the end, it is the act of giving back that truly enriches our lives and leaves a lasting legacy of compassion and generosity.

GRATITUDE IN LEADERSHIP:
How Successful CEOs Harness Thankfulness

In the realm of leadership, where strategic decision-making and vision setting take center stage, one often overlooked yet powerful quality stands out: gratitude. Successful CEOs understand that expressing thankfulness is not merely a polite gesture but a transformative leadership tool. In this article, we delve into the role of gratitude in effective leadership, drawing insights from the practices of renowned CEOs.

Gratitude as a Leadership Trait: Gratitude is more than a mere emotion; it is a leadership trait that fosters positive workplace cultures and drives organizational success. When CEOs cultivate a culture of gratitude within their companies, they set the stage for increased employee engagement, motivation, and loyalty. Recognizing and appreciating the efforts of their teams creates an environment where individuals feel valued and empowered.

Gratitude as a Leadership Trait:
Gratitude is more than a mere emotion; it is a leadership trait that fosters positive workplace cultures and drives organizational success. When CEOs cultivate a culture of gratitude within their companies, they set the stage for increased employee engagement, motivation, and loyalty. Recognizing and appreciating the efforts of their teams creates an environment where individuals feel valued and empowered.

LEADING BY EXAMPLE:

DThe most influential CEOs lead by example when it comes to expressing gratitude. They understand that their actions and attitudes set the tone for the entire organization. By showing appreciation for their employees' contributions, they inspire a sense of pride and purpose within the team. This, in turn, leads to higher levels of commitment and productivity.

The Ripple Effect: Gratitude in leadership has a ripple effect that extends far beyond the CEO's office. When leaders express thankfulness openly and consistently, it encourages employees to do the same. This creates a positive feedback loop where gratitude becomes an integral part of the organizational culture. As a result, employees are more likely to recognize and appreciate their colleagues, fostering a supportive and collaborative work environment.

Enhancing Decision-Making: Gratitude also plays a role in decision-making. CEOs who practice gratitude are more attuned to the needs and concerns of their employees. They consider the impact of their decisions on the workforce and strive to make choices that benefit both the company and its people. This approach not only leads to more ethical decision-making but also enhances the overall reputation and success of the organization.

Gratitude and Innovation: Innovative thinking is another area where gratitude in leadership shines. CEOs who appreciate the diverse talents and perspectives of their teams are more likely to foster an environment where creativity and innovation thrive. They understand that by acknowledging and valuing different viewpoints, they can unlock new solutions and opportunities for growth.

Conclusion: In the world of leadership, gratitude is a powerful yet often underestimated tool. Successful CEOs harness the potential of thankfulness to create positive workplace cultures, inspire their teams, and drive organizational success. By leading with gratitude, they set a precedent that fosters loyalty, collaboration, and innovation. As we look to the future of leadership, let us recognize the transformative role that gratitude can play in guiding organizations toward greater prosperity and purpose.

Healthy Brussel Sprout Salad

Ingredients

5 cups brussel sprout, shaved
⅕ cup olive oil
⅕ cup lemon juice
1 cup roasted walnut
½ cup dried berries of your choosing
⅓ cup ricotta cheese shaved
Salt and pepper

Directions

1. Slice the brussel sprout using mandoline, set aside
2. Wash the sliced brussel sprout, and let it dry with vegetable drier
3. Mix brussel sprout, lemon juice, walnut, dried berries, and cheese into a bowl and toss it
4. Drizzle with olive oil

Tips:
You can always use different nuts or mixed grain to add more texture
Adding more crunchy vegetable will result in complex taste

ZUCCHINI & TOFU SCAMPI

VEGAN · 4 SERVINGS · 30 MIN

INGREDIENTS

- 4 medium zucchinis
- 1 tablespoon oil
- 1/4 lb tofu
- 1 teaspoon salt
- ½ teaspoon black pepper
- ½ teaspoon red pepper flakes
- 3 cloves garlic, minced
- ¼ cup low-sodium broth
- 1 lemon, juiced
- fresh parsley, for garnish

DIRECTIONS

1. Using a coarse cheese grater, slide the zucchini down the grater, shaving off long strips.
2. Heat the oil over medium-high heat in a large, nonstick skillet.
3. Add the shrimp in and season with salt, black pepper, red pepper, and garlic. Sauté the tofu
4. Add the zucchini noodles and stir until everything is combined and the shrimp are fully cooked.
5. Sprinkle with chopped fresh parsley leaves and serve

NOTES

Green Bean Casserole

Ingredients

- 1 1/2 pounds fresh green beans, trimmed and cut into bite-sized pieces
- 1 can (10.5 ounces) condensed cream of mushroom soup
- 1 cup milk
- 1 teaspoon soy sauce
- 1/2 teaspoon garlic powder
- 1/4 teaspoon black pepper
- 1 1/3 cups French-fried onions

Directions

1. Preheat the Oven: Preheat your oven to 350°F (175°C).
2. Blanch the Green Beans: Bring a large pot of water to a boil. Add the green beans and blanch them for about 2-3 minutes until they are bright green and slightly tender. Drain the beans and immediately transfer them to a bowl of ice water to stop the cooking process. Drain again and set aside.
3. Prepare the Sauce: In a separate bowl, mix together the condensed cream of mushroom soup, milk, soy sauce, garlic powder, and black pepper. Stir until the mixture is well combined.
4. Combine Green Beans and Sauce: In a large mixing bowl, combine the blanched green beans with the mushroom soup mixture. Stir until the green beans are evenly coated with the sauce.
5. Transfer to a Casserole Dish: Pour the green bean mixture into a greased 9x13-inch baking dish or a similar-sized casserole dish.
6. Bake: Place the casserole dish in the preheated oven and bake for 25-30 minutes or until the mixture is heated through and bubbly.
7. Add Crispy Onions: Remove the casserole from the oven and sprinkle the French-fried onions evenly over the top.
8. Bake Again: Return the casserole to the oven and bake for an additional 5-10 minutes, or until the onions are crispy and golden brown.
9. Serve: Remove the casserole from the oven and let it cool for a few minutes before serving. Enjoy your creamy and crispy Green Bean Casserole!

CHICKEN TIKKA MASALA

INGREDIENTS

- For the Chicken Marinade:
- 1 1/2 pounds boneless, skinless chicken breasts or thighs, cut into bite-sized pieces
- 1 cup plain yogurt
- 2 tablespoons lemon juice
- 2 teaspoons ground cumin
- 2 teaspoons ground coriander
- 1 teaspoon ground turmeric
- 1 teaspoon paprika
- 1 teaspoon garam masala
- 1 teaspoon chili powder (adjust to taste)
- 2 teaspoons minced garlic
- 2 teaspoons minced ginger
- Salt and pepper to taste
- For the Sauce:
- 2 tablespoons vegetable oil or ghee
- 1 large onion, finely chopped
- 2 teaspoons minced garlic
- 2 teaspoons minced ginger
- 1 teaspoon ground cumin
- 1 teaspoon ground coriander
- 1 teaspoon paprika
- 1 teaspoon turmeric
- 1 teaspoon garam masala
- 1/2 teaspoon chili powder (adjust to taste)
- 1 can (14 ounces) crushed tomatoes
- 1 cup heavy cream
- Salt and pepper to taste
- Fresh cilantro leaves for garnish (optional)

DIRECTIONS

1. Marinate the Chicken:
2. In a large bowl, combine the yogurt, lemon juice, cumin, coriander, turmeric, paprika, garam masala, chili powder, minced garlic, minced ginger, salt, and pepper. Mix well.
3. Add the chicken pieces to the marinade and coat them thoroughly. Cover the bowl and refrigerate for at least 1 hour, or preferably overnight for the best flavor.
4. Cook the Chicken:
5. Preheat your grill or broiler. Thread the marinated chicken pieces onto skewers and grill or broil until they are cooked through and slightly charred. This should take about 5-7 minutes per side.
6. Remove the cooked chicken from the skewers and set aside.
7. Prepare the Sauce:
8. In a large skillet or saucepan, heat the vegetable oil or ghee over medium heat. Add the chopped onion and sauté until it becomes translucent and starts to brown.
9. Add the minced garlic and ginger to the skillet and cook for another 2 minutes until fragrant.
10. Stir in the ground cumin, ground coriander, paprika, turmeric, garam masala, and chili powder. Cook for an additional 2 minutes to toast the spices.
11. Pour in the crushed tomatoes and bring the mixture to a simmer. Cook for about 10 minutes, stirring occasionally, until the sauce thickens.
12. Stir in the heavy cream and cooked chicken pieces. Simmer for another 10-15 minutes, allowing the flavors to meld together.
13. Season the sauce with salt and pepper to taste.
14. Serve:
15. Garnish the Chicken Tikka Masala with fresh cilantro leaves if desired.
16. Serve the Chicken Tikka Masala hot over cooked rice or with naan bread. Enjoy your delicious homemade Chicken Tikka Masala!

www.ingramcontent.com/pod-product-compliance
Lightning Source LLC
LaVergne TN
LVRC080725070526
838199LV00042B/740